D1649878

A STUDIO PRESS BOOK

First published in the UK in 2020 by Studio Press,
an imprint of Bonnier Books UK,
The Plaza, 535 King's Road, London SW10 0SZ
Owned by Bonnier Books,
Sveavägen 56, Stockholm, Sweden

www.studiopressbooks.co.uk
www.bonnierbooks.co.uk

1 3 5 7 9 10 8 6 4 2

ISBN 978-1-78741-905-6

Written by Stephanie Milton
Designed by Rob Ward and Wendy Bartlet
Production by Emma Kidd
Special thanks to Chris Milton and Heather Blakey

A CIP catalogue for this book is available from the British Library

Printed and bound in Poland

THE ULTIMATE GUIDE TO

Animal Crossing

NEW HORIZONS

100% UNOFFICIAL

CONTENTS

WELCOME, RESIDENT!

Welcome to the ultimate guide to Animal Crossing: New Horizons! Congratulations on signing up to a deserted island getaway package – you've made a great decision.

Your new life will be all about community and creativity. There's so much to discover on your deserted island, so we've created this handy guide to help you make the most of your time there. We'll show you how to make friends, gather crafting materials and recipes, learn about the island's wildlife, enjoy the seasons, decorate your home and develop your own little island paradise. With the help of this guide, you'll be the proud owner of a five star island in no time.

Let's have some fun, shall we?

WELCOME TO YOUR ISLAND

Welcome to your island! This little piece of land is yours to develop however you like. But before we get creative, let's meet a few people and learn a bit about the adventure that awaits you.

TIMMY AND TOMMY NOOK

This tanuki duo work for Nook Inc, and they're the first people you'll meet on your adventure. They're here to welcome you to your island and help you to get set up. Once you're settled on the island, they'll open a shop called Nook's Cranny, selling a variety of homewares and garden supplies. You'll never see one without the other – they do everything together.

Nook Inc. Deserted Island Getaway Package
Paquete de escapada a islas desiertas

Timmy

Welcome... to the check-in counter for your Deserted Island Getaway package!

TOM NOOK

Tom Nook is a business tycoon and head of Nook Inc. He runs Resident Services and the development of the island is his number one goal. If you're ever unsure what to do, Tom will have a suggestion for you – he can be found at Resident Services.

DID YOU KNOW? For the moment, Resident Services is a simple green tent, but soon you'll be able to upgrade to a proper Town Hall. If you need help with anything or want to speak to Tom, this is the place to come.

YOUR TENT

Timmy and Tom will give you a tent on your first night. Choose where to pitch it carefully – although you can move your home later on, it will cost you lots of Bells (the island's currency).

I set up my tent!
That's a big first step!

VILLAGERS

Your first two villagers will arrive with you on the flight. Once you develop the island, you'll be able to invite more villagers to live there. You'll be asked to help your first two villagers choose spots for their tents as well – again, choose carefully, because moving their homes later will cost Bells.

Agnes

I can't believe I got such an awesome spot. You rock, snuffle!

NAMING YOUR ISLAND

You can't change this later, so take your time to find the right name. Although everyone gets a vote, the name you suggest will be the name that's chosen. At this point you'll become the island's Resident Representative – congratulations!

Tom Nook

Splendid! Then from now on, this island will be known as Moonstone.

ISABELLE

Good morning, everyone!

Isabelle won't move to your island until you upgrade the Resident Services tent and open the Town Hall. One of Animal Crossing's most popular characters, she represents all that is good in the world – she's helpful, sweet, and always knows what's going on.

YOUR NOOK PHONE

11:25 AM
Camera

On your second day, Tom will give you your very own Nook Phone. It's programmed with several handy apps right off the bat, and soon you'll have access to even more apps. It has a Nook Miles app to help you track and earn miles, a Critterpedia to tell you about the bugs and fish you've discovered, a camera so you can capture memories, and much more!

DID YOU KNOW?

Bells are the island's currency and can be used to buy items in the shops. Nook Miles are an achievement-based currency and you earn miles simply by living your life. Check your Nook Miles app to see which activities reward you with Miles.

IMPORTANT EARLY ACHIEVEMENTS

Animal Crossing can be slow to get going, but if you do these things as soon as you can, it will help you to progress to the good stuff as quickly as possible. Try to prioritise these tasks and tick them off your list asap.

1 ## TAKE FIVE BUGS TO TOM AT RESIDENT SERVICES

Tom will send them to his good friend Blathers. This will convince Blathers to move to the island in order to research its wildlife.

Tom Nook

An old friend of mine runs a museum, and I'd love to send it to him for a closer look.

2 ## TAKE 15 UNIQUE ITEMS TO BLATHERS

Take 15 unique items to Blathers as soon as you can – these can be fish, bugs or fossils. Once you've done this, he'll decide to open a museum.

Blathers

If I am to open the museum, I must acquire more items to exhibit... 15 more, to be precise.

3 ## GET THE POCKET ORGANISATION TOOL

This expands your inventory to 30 slots. Just head to the Nook Stop multimedia terminal – it'll cost you 5,000 Nook Miles.

4 GATHER CONSTRUCTION MATERIALS FOR NOOK'S CRANNY

Speak to Timmy in the Resident Services tent – he'll ask you to collect wood and iron to build the shop.

5 CONSTRUCT YOUR FIRST THREE HOUSES

Go and see Tom – he'll tell you to build three new houses and a bridge to attract more villagers.

Tom Nook
Hello? That you, Steph? Yes, yes, this is Tom Nook! How goes your search for housing land?

6 UPGRADE RESIDENT SERVICES

Once the next three villagers have moved in, Tom will announce his plans to upgrade the Resident Services tent to the Town Hall. Once it's open you'll be able to start developing more plots of land for villagers – you can have up to ten resident villagers, not including yourself. If you want to have some control over who moves in, now's the time to start visiting mystery islands. More about that on pages 80–85.

7 GET THE ULTIMATE POCKET STUFFING TOOL

This expands your inventory to its maximum 40 slots – you get it by redeeming 8,000 Nook Miles at the Nook Stop multimedia terminal in the Town Hall.

Axe

22,743

TIME AND SEASONS

*Time in Animal Crossing is in sync with time in real life –
the day and night cycle is the same, and you can experience
the seasons in the same way you would in the real world.
One thing's for sure: nothing stays the same for very long
in this game. That's what makes it interesting!*

NORTHERN AND SOUTHERN HEMISPHERE ISLANDS

When you first embark on your adventure, you'll be asked to choose either
a Northern or Southern Hemisphere island. For the purposed of this guide,
we've chosen a Northern Hemisphere island, which means summer is June
to August and winter is December to February.

WEATHER

The weather in Animal Crossing is no less unpredictable than the weather in real life, but that's what makes it fun, right? You'll wake up one day to cloudless blue skies, and the next it will pour with rain from sunrise to sunset. But terrible weather isn't all bad news – certain bugs only appear when it rains, and you're more likely to get rare fish, too. Sometimes you'll even see a rainbow.

TIME OF DAY

It's worth checking in on your island at different times throughout the day and night. Some things only happen at night – you'll only see Wisp and meteor showers after 7pm. Sunrise and sunset are beautiful – make sure to snap some pictures.

SEASONS

Each season brings new treats – this is a game you'll want to stick with for the long-term. Bugs and fish are seasonal, and items like pinecones, cherry blossom and snowflakes only appear at certain times of the year.

SEASONAL EVENTS CALENDAR

There are seasonal events to look forward to all year round. Each event offers you the opportunity to make lots of Bells and earn rare items. Here's a calendar of some of the most exciting events – you won't want to miss these!

JANUARY

- Bug Off
  (Southern Hemisphere)
- Fishing Tourney

FEBRUARY

- Bug Off
  (Southern Hemisphere)

MARCH

- Nothing to report at present – watch this space!

APRIL

- Bunny Day
- Fishing Tourney
- Earth Day

C.J.

YES! Nobody can resist the siren song of the Fishing Tourney.

MAY

- May Day
- International Museum Day

JUNE

- Wedding Season
- Bug Off (Northern Hemisphere)

JULY

- Fishing Tourney
- Bug Off (Northern Hemisphere)

AUGUST

- Fireworks Show
- Bug Off (Northern Hemisphere)

SEPTEMBER

- Bug Off
  (Northern Hemisphere)

Rule number one: catch as many bugs as you can within 3 minutes!

OCTOBER

- Fishing Tourney
- Halloween

NOVEMBER

- Bug Off (Southern Hemisphere)
- Harvest Festival

DECEMBER

- Bug Off (Southern Hemisphere)
- Toy Day

YOUR HOME

You'll start your adventure in a simple tent, but you'll soon be able to upgrade to a house, which can be expanded multiple times. You can also customise the exterior of your house. All it takes is a bit of hard work and a LOT of Bells.

EXPANDING YOUR HOME

Go and see Tom when you're ready to upgrade your home. Each time you expand, the cost increases until the loan amounts are eye-wateringly high. Here's a guide to every step of the process, from tent to mansion.

1 **UPGRADING YOUR TENT TO A HOUSE**

Cost: 98,000 Bells

4 **ADDING A ROOM ON THE LEFT**

Cost: 548,000 Bells

2

INCREASING THE SIZE OF YOUR ROOM

Cost: 198,000 Bells

3

ADDING A BACK ROOM

Cost: 348,000 Bells

DID YOU KNOW? Houses have built-in storage slots where you can stash items you aren't using right now. Each time you expand your house, your storage increases along with it.

6 ADDING A SECOND FLOOR ROOM

Cost: 1,248,000 Bells

7 ADDING A BASEMENT

Cost: 2,498,000 Bells

5 ADDING A ROOM ON THE RIGHT

Cost: 758,000 Bells

CUSTOMISING THE EXTERIOR

You can change everything from the front door and mailbox to the roof. The cost is 5,000 Bells and Tom has a catalogue of styles for you to choose from.

MOVING YOUR HOUSE

At some point, you may decide that a clifftop house is essential to your happiness. For 30,000 Bells, Tom will move your house – just let him know, find a spot and the next day your house will have a new home.

TREES

There are two native trees on your island – cedar trees and one type of fruit tree. Your native fruit will be apple, cherry, orange, peach or pear. Don't worry – you'll be able to find all the other kinds of fruit trees eventually, as well as coconut trees! But how can trees help you? Let's take a look.

BRANCHES

Trees drop branches. You'll want to gather these up as you'll need them to craft flimsy tools and other items. Branches will drop from trees on their own, but you can also shake trees to release more.

Tree branch

FURNITURE AND BELLS

Every day, two of your island's trees will have a piece of furniture hidden in them. Shake each tree on your island until they drop out. Some trees also contain 100-Bell coins!

100 Bells

FRUIT

Shake fruit trees or chop them once with an axe and they'll drop their fruit. Fruit can be sold at Nook's Cranny, or used to craft items like housewares and clothing. The fruit will grow back in three days.

WASPS' NESTS

I caught a wasp! That's gotta sting...

Unfortunately, some trees also contain wasps' nests. When the nest falls out, an angry swarm of wasps will start chasing you. Always have your net in your hand when you shake trees – if you're quick, you can catch the swarm before they sting you.

WASP STINGS

Being stung by a wasp is not a good look. Get stung again while you're still suffering from a sting and you'll faint – you'll wake up back at your house. You can craft or buy medicine to cure a wasp sting. Kind villagers might also give you medicine if they see the state you're in.

Ow! Ow ow ow... I got stung by wasps!

TREE-LOVING BUGS

There are several bugs that like to live in trees or on their trunks. Some are worth an impressive 12,000 Bells! They can be captured with a net, but you'll need to be sneaky – for more info on bugs, see pages 38–43.

Softwood

WOOD

Chop trees with an axe and you'll get wood – an essential crafting ingredient. You can chop a tree three times with a flimsy axe without chopping it down, but an axe will demolish the tree on the third strike.

TREE STUMPS

When you chop down a tree you'll be left with a stump. You can dig this up with a shovel if you like, but stumps make handy seats and also attracts certain insects like the rosalia batesi – a valuable beetle worth 3,000 Bells.

PLANTING TREES

You can plant fruit or saplings to grow trees – saplings are on sale at Nook's Cranny. Trees will only grow if they have enough space, so choose a spot with space all around it. Make sure it's not right up against a cliff or right next to water.

MOVING TREES

If you want to move a fully grown tree, you'll need to eat some fruit. This will give you 'fruit power' – a magical ability to dig up entire trees with your shovel. Eat one piece of fruit for each tree you want to move. A fruit power counter will appear in the top left of your screen and you can eat a maximum of 10 pieces.

COCONUT TREES

When you start visiting mystery islands using Nook Miles tickets, you'll be able to collect coconuts. Bring these home and plant them on your beaches to grow your very own coconut trees.

FLOWERS

Flowers are a lovely way to bring even more natural beauty to your island. As well as attracting bugs and adding a bit of colour, flowers can also be used to craft fun, floral-themed items. Here's everything you need to know about Animal Crossing's beautiful blooms.

NATIVE FLOWERS

There are eight flower species: cosmos, hyacinths, lilies, mums, pansies, roses, tulips and windflowers. Your island has one native flower, which you'll find growing on your cliffs – this flower will always be available for you to buy at Nook's Cranny, too. Your native flower will grow naturally in three colours, usually red, white and yellow.

NON-NATIVE FLOWERS

You can buy non-native flower species from Leif when he visits your island, and there will also be a rotating selection available from Nook's Cranny. You can also gather them when you visit friends' islands or mystery islands.

SPECIAL GUEST APPEARANCE – LEIF

Another familiar face for Animal Crossing fans, Leif the sloth appears in the plaza every so often, selling flowers and shrubs. He'll even pay for your weeds, beating Timmy and Tommy Nook's price.

TIP

Make sure you water your flowers regularly – you can earn Nook Miles for tending to them.

DID YOU KNOW?

Flowers help to increase your island's rating so it's a good idea to plant lots – find out more on page 126.

BREEDING HYBRID FLOWERS

Feeling green-fingered? You can breed hybrid flowers in a range of unusual hues, from black to blue. Breeding hybrid flowers is all about positioning. Here's a handy guide showing you the most efficient way to breed each flower in order to produce hybrid colours.

TIP

You'll need to water flowers in order to breed them, so get yourself a watering can if you haven't already got one. You'll know a flower is watered and ready for breeding if it sparkles.

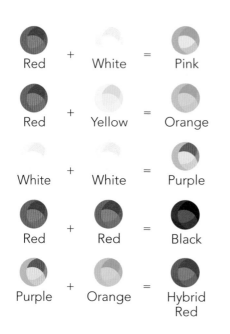

Red + White = Pink

Red + Yellow = Orange

White + White = Purple

Red + Red = Black

Purple + Orange = Hybrid Red

ROSES

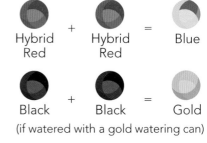

Hybrid Red + Hybrid Red = Blue

Black + Black = Gold

(if watered with a gold watering can)

26

TULIPS

 Red + White = Pink

 Orange + Orange = Purple

Red + Yellow = Orange

Red + Red = Black

Black + Black = Purple

WINDFLOWERS

 Red + Orange = Pink

White + White = Blue

Blue + Blue = Purple

Blue + Pink = Purple

DID YOU KNOW? You'll get a gold watering can as a reward for achieving five star island status. See page 157 for more info.

PANSIES

 Red + Yellow = Orange

 Hybrid Red + Hybrid Red = Purple

White + White = Blue

 Hybrid Orange + Hybrid Orange = Purple

 Blue + Red = Hybrid Red

 Orange + Blue = Hybrid Orange

 Blue + Blue = Purple

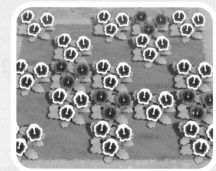

COSMOS

 Red + White = Pink

 Red + Yellow = Orange

  Red + Red = Black

 Orange + Orange = Black

HYACINTHS

 Red + Yellow = Orange

 Red + White = Pink

White + White = Blue

 Orange + Orange = Purple

LILIES

 Red + White = Pink

Red + Yellow = Orange

Red + Red = Black

 Red + White = Pink

White + White = Purple

Purple + Purple = Green

MUMS

DID YOU KNOW? Although these are the most efficient ways to breed hybrid colours, there are other combinations that will work, so have fun experimenting.

29

SHRUBS

Well-placed shrubs can really help to elevate your island décor. They can be purchased from Leif's stand on the plaza. Shrubs only flower when they're in season, and the flowering period is different for each variety. So, whatever time of year it is, there'll always be something in bloom.

HOW TO PLANT SHRUBS

Shrubs can be planted in the same way as flowers and trees: pick a spot, dig a hole with your shovel and plant your shrub of choice. It'll be a few days before your shrub reaches full size, and it will only produce flowers if it's the right season.

DID YOU KNOW? Unlike flowers, shrubs don't need to be watered. They're super low maintenance!

HOW TO USE SHRUBS

You can't walk through shrubs in the same way that you can walk through flowers. This means you can use shrubs to make attractive borders between different areas of your island. Since shrubs only flower for a brief period each year, they'll look like hedges most of the time.

DID YOU KNOW? Snails love shrubs – you'll see them sitting on top of the leaves on rainy days.

SHRUB VARIETIES

CAMELLIA
Available in pink and red, camellias bloom from early February to late March.

HYDRANGEAS
Available in blue and pink, hydrangeas flower from early June to mid-July.

TEA OLIVES
Available in orange and yellow, tea olives flower from late September to late October.

AZALIAS
Available in white or pink, azalias flower from mid-April to late May.

HIBISCUS
Available in red and yellow, hibiscuses bloom from late July to mid-September.

HOLLY
Holly blooms from early November to late December.

ROCKS

Your island is home to six large rocks. Now, they may not look very interesting at first glance, but they're a source of rare materials, attract rare bugs and even produce Bells! So grab your shovel and let's find out what they have to offer.

STRIKING ROCKS

Rocks can be struck up to eight times with a shovel to release their contents. There's a time limit once you start striking a rock, and you'll be knocked backwards each time you hit it – you'll usually only manage seven items before the time runs out.

BRACING YOURSELF

If you dig holes behind you first, this will stop you being knocked backwards and, if you're quick, you should be able to collect all eight drops. Make sure there are no flowers or items in the area around the rock, otherwise it won't drop everything.

TIP

Don't like where a rock is positioned? Eat a piece of fruit to give you fruit power, then hit it with your shovel to break it. It will appear the following day in a different spot.

MATERIALS

Gold nugget

Rocks drop stones, iron nuggets and clay – all essential crafting ingredients. Very occasionally, a rock will drop a gold nugget. These are used to craft a number of rare and valuable items, such as zodiac-themed items and golden tools – the very best tools in the game. If you're desperate for cash, you can also sell gold nuggets for 10,000 Bells apiece, but we'd highly recommend you hold on to them.

THE MONEY ROCK

Each day, one of your island's rocks will be a money rock, which means it will drop Bells instead of crafting materials. If you use the bracing trick, you'll be able to grab 15,800 Bells each day.

ROCK-LOVING BUGS

Some bugs just love rocks! You might see a snail sitting on top of a rock, or spot a critter crawling away after you strike a rock. Learn more about bugs on pages 38–43.

CRAFTING

A great addition to Animal Crossing, crafting gives you more scope to bring fun items into your life. Here are our top tips to help you make the most of this addictive activity.

COLLECTING RECIPES

A message bottle containing a crafting recipe will wash up somewhere on your beach each day. You can buy recipes for equipment like shovels in Nook's Cranny, as well as some collections of recipes. If you visit a villager's home and they're in the middle of crafting something, they'll share the recipe with you. You might also get a recipe inside a balloon – see pages 60–61. Some rare recipes are only available if you redeem Nook Miles.

Whitney

I know! Why don't you try making a cosmos shower too?

LEARNING RECIPES

You have to learn recipes before you can craft items. Open your inventory and select the recipe card – it will give you the option to learn it. If it's a recipe you already know, you can sell it at Nook's Cranny or give it to a friend.

SWEET! I learned a DIY recipe for a cardboard table!

CRAFTING WORKBENCHES

To craft an item, you'll need a workbench. There are four available to craft and you can also buy a cute DIY table from Nook's Cranny. When you interact with a crafting workbench, it will show you all the recipes you know. If you have the required materials, there will be a 'craftable' stamp on the recipe.

CUSTOMISING ITEMS

Some items can also be customised at a crafting bench, which means you can change their appearance. You'll need to purchase customisation kits from Nook's Cranny.

I customised a potted ivy!

TIP

Most people set up their crafting workbench near their home, but it can be quite time-consuming to keep running back and forth from your house whenever you want to craft items. Make things easier on yourself and set up multiple crafting benches across the island.

FOSSILS

If you've played any of the previous Animal Crossing games, you'll know all about fossils. These items can be displayed in your museum or sold for Bells at Nook's Cranny.

HOW TO FIND FOSSILS

Each day, four to six new fossils will appear on your island. They're buried in the ground and look like star-shaped holes. They can be retrieved by digging up the spot with a shovel.

Look! I dug up
a fossil!

TIP

You might also find fossils on mystery islands, so make sure you take a shovel.

GETTING FOSSILS APPRAISED

Blathers

Coprolites are, in fact... ehm... bits of fossilised... feces. Hoo! Eew! It's true!

Fossils must be appraised by Blathers at the museum. Since Blathers knows absolutely everything, he always has some fun facts to share with you about your finds.

THE MUSEUM FOSSIL WING

You can donate one of each kind of fossil to the museum – any duplicates can be sold for Bells at Nook's Cranny. There are 73 fossils in total – if you want to see which fossils you already have, check Nook Shopping at the Nook Stop in the Town Hall. That way, you'll have an idea of how many you need to complete the museum's fossil wing.

SELLING FOSSILS

If you have spare fossils, Timmy and Tommy will happily take them off your hands. They're worth anything between 1,000 and 6,000 Bells.

Timmy

A T. rex skull! Sure! How about if I offer you 6,000 Bells?

BUGS

Assuming you're not as scared of bugs as Blathers is, you're in for a real treat – bugs are fascinating! Like fossils, you can donate bugs to the museum, and they're worth Bells, too. The trick is knowing where to find them and then employing your sneakiest tactics to capture them. Grab your net and let's get bug hunting!

TIP

Don't forget to check your Critterpedia to find out all about your latest catch. It'll also tell you whether you need to donate it to the museum.

SPECIAL GUEST APPEARANCE – FLICK

Flick is a chameleon with a deep love of bugs. He'll visit your island every so often and offer to buy your bugs for 150% of the price you'd get at Nook's Cranny. He can also make a model of your favourite bug if you bring him three of them. It's worth saving your best bugs for his visits.

So if you find a bug, will you sell it to me? I can pay a little extra... no price is too high for my chitinous kindred!

FLYING BUGS

You'll see lots of bugs flying around your island, from bees to dragonflies. Some, like the mosquito, are simply annoying. Others, like the emperor butterfly, are beautiful and majestic. Some are extremely rare – fireflies can only be seen in June for Northern Hemisphere islands and December for Southern Hemisphere islands.

I caught an emperor butterfly! It's not your average monarch!

BUGS THAT LIKE ROCKS

I caught a centipede! 99 more and I'll have a dollarpede!

There are currently three bugs that like to hang out on rocks – snails, pill bugs and centipedes. Snails perch atop rocks in rainy weather. Pill bugs and centipedes will only emerge when you strike the rock, and you'll need to be quick with your net if you want to catch them.

BUGS THAT LIKE FLOWERS

Some bugs are happiest living amongst the flowers. Ladybugs can be seen flying around blooms and man-faced stinkbugs can be seen crawling across their surface. The orchid mantis is particularly choosy – it will only crawl around on white flowers.

I caught an orchid mantis! Our friendship is blooming!

BUGS THAT LIKE TREES

Some bugs love nothing more than hanging out on tree trunks or hiding in amongst the leaves. The trunk-loving bugs come in all shapes and sizes, from small beetles and cicadas to giant atlas moths. The leaf-loving bugs like spiders and bagworms won't appear unless you shake the tree – then they'll hang down from the branches for you to capture them with your net.

I caught a spider! I spied 'er first!

BUGS THAT LIKE TREE STUMPS

I caught a rosalia batesi beetle!
That's easier to do than say!

It's worth leaving a few tree stumps around your island as they will attract bugs like the violin beetle, the jewel beetle and the rosalia batesi beetle. The rosalia batesi can be sold for 3,000 Bells, but you'll have to be sneaky and approach it very slowly.

DID YOU KNOW? In order to catch bugs on rocks, flowers and trees, you'll need to use the sneak function – just press and hold A whilst holding your net before you approach a bug, then release A when you're ready to pounce. If you don't sneak up on them, they'll flee before you can get there.

GROUND BUGS

Ground bugs include everything from ants and grasshoppers to walking leaf bugs disguised as dropped items. Some will be frequent visitors to your island, others have very specific requirements – ants are attracted to rotten turnips, for example, and flies are attracted to trash items.

I caught a walking leaf!
It seems to be taking
it in stride!

DID YOU KNOW? Bugs are seasonal and will only appear during certain months. Check your Critterpedia for details.

TARANTULAS AND SCORPIONS

You'll only ever see these ground bugs at night, when they're in season. Tarantulas appear between November and April, and scorpions between May and October. Both are very quick and venomous – one bite and you'll faint. You'll have to be as quick as they are if you want to catch them. The key to catching a tarantula is to approach with your net raised, then wait until it lowers its legs to release your net. To catch a scorpion, wait until it freezes, then quickly rush it with your net and hope for the best. They're worth 8,000 Bells each, so can make brave islanders a lot of money.

I caught a scorpion! It was a sting operation!

DONATING BUGS TO THE MUSEUM

If there's one thing Blathers detests, it's bugs. Oh, he'll still accept them, devoted as he is to the museum's development, but he'll be most uncomfortable about it. When he asks you if you wish to know more about your bug,

Blathers

Perhaps I've picked the wrong profession.

you have one of two options: let him off the hook if you're feeling kind, or take him up on the offer if you fancy a laugh – his descriptions are very funny.

MUSEUM BUG HOUSE

Make sure to visit the museum bug house once you've donated a few specimens. Blathers takes very good care of them – it's set up to provide them with everything they could possibly want.

SELLING BUGS

Selling duplicate bugs can make you a lot of Bells. Try to hold onto them until Flick visits to get the best price. The most valuable bugs are also the rarest – golden stags, giraffe stags and horned hercules go for 12,000 bells each, and giant stags and scarab beetles go for 10,000 Bells each.

Tommy

A horned elephant!
Sure! How about if I offer you
8,000 Bells?

BEACHCOMBING

You'll find all sorts of things on your beaches each day, from shells and message bottles to rare creatures. Make sure you comb your beaches each day and grab these things when you see them.

SHELLS

Coral

Shells can be sold at Nook's Cranny or used to craft shell-themed homewares. The most valuable are giant clams, which sell for 900 Bells, conches, which sell for 700 Bells and scallop and summer shells, both of which sell for 600 Bells. As their name suggests, summer shells are only available in summer – they can be used to craft shell-themed items like the shell wreath.

MANILLA CLAMS

Visible as spurts of water erupting from the sand, manilla clams can be used to craft fish bait. They can also be sold for 100 Bells each.

I got a manilla clam! Manilla is my favourite flavour of clam!

WHARF ROACHES

Seen scurrying about on rocks, wharf roaches can be donated to the museum and sold for 200 Bells each.

I caught a wharf roach! This water-loving roach has no pier!

HERMIT CRABS

Hermit crabs look like sea shells, but get close to them and they'll attempt to scurry off. If you're quick, you can catch them in a net before they disappear into the sea. They can be donated to the museum and sold for 1,000 Bells.

I caught a hermit crab! I think it wanted to be left alone!

MESSAGE BOTTLE

Every day, a message bottle will wash up somewhere on your beaches. Inside, along with a note, you'll find a crafting recipe. If it's a recipe you already know, you can sell it at Nook's Cranny for 200 Bells.

Message bottle

FISH

Fishing can be a little tricky, but some fish are incredibly valuable, so it's a skill worth perfecting. Freshwater fish are found in rivers and ponds, and saltwater fish are found in the sea. Altogether, there are 80 different fish to catch – you can donate them to the museum and sell them for Bells. All you need is a fishing rod, and perhaps some fish bait.

TIP

Like bugs, fish are catalogued in your Critterpedia as you catch them. Don't forget to check it out to learn more about your latest catch.

SPECIAL GUEST APPEARANCE – CJ

Oh, you got a whole school for me? Altogether that'll be... 16,200 Bells. Deal?

CJ the beaver is obsessed with fish. He'll appear on your island every so often to set you one of his infamous seasports challenges. Complete the challenge and he'll offer to buy your fish for 1.5 times what Timmy and Tommy will pay. Save three of your favourites and he'll get his partner, Flick, to craft them into a model for you.

CATCHING FISH

I caught a piranha!
Sure hope it was the only one!

Look for a fish shadow in a body of water. The shadow may be tiny, small, medium, large, extra large or huge, and this gives you an indication of the size the fish will be. Cast your fishing rod in front of a fish by pressing A and wait for it to approach. It will nibble at the bobber a couple of times before latching on – at this point, the bobber will dip below the water and you'll hear a loud plopping sound. Press and hold A quickly to reel it in.

TIP

Struggling to catch fish? Close your eyes and concentrate on the sound of the bobber instead of watching the fish. You can also craft bait out of manilla clams and scatter it in the water.

DONATING FISH TO THE MUSEUM

Blathers will happily accept one of each kind of fish for the museum aquarium. Make sure you visit regularly to see how it's coming along – it's a great place to relax and take a moment for yourself whilst marvelling at the different species.

SELLING FISH

Selling fish is one of the best ways to make Bells – many species are worth in excess of 10,000 Bells each. You can sell them at Nook's Cranny, but, to get maximum profit, try to hang onto them until CJ's visiting. Here are some of the most valuable fish to keep an eye out for.

SAW SHARK

Location: sea
Shadow size: huge
with fin
Price: 12,000 Bells

I caught a saw shark!
You could call it a sea saw!

Thar she blows!

WHALE SHARK

Location: sea
Shadow size: huge
with fin
Price: 13,000 Bells

DORADO

Location: river
Shadow size: extra
large
Price: 15,000 Bells

I caught a dorado!
I say "dorado", you say "doraydo".

BARRELEYE

Location: sea
Shadow size: small
Price: 15,000 Bells

I caught a barreleye!
Like eyeing fish in a barrel!

Blast from the past!

COELACANTH

Location: sea, only
when raining
Shadow size: huge
Price: 15,000 Bells

GREAT WHITE SHARK

Location: sea
Shadow size: huge
with fin
Price: 15,000 Bells

I caught a great white shark!
Watch out for its jaws!

DID YOU KNOW? Certain rare fish will only appear at the end of your pier, so don't forget to fish around that area, too.

SEA CREATURES

Thanks to the Swimming Update, the waters around your island are now home to everything from pretty pearls to vampire squid. Collecting sea creatures is another great way to fill your museum and make Bells, as well as to gather the materials you need to craft mermaid-themed items.

SWIMMING GEAR

If you want to swim, you'll need a wet suit. You can purchase one from Nook's Cranny – just take a look in the cabinet. Nintendo will kindly send you a free snorkel through the post, and you can also redeem your Nook Miles for a Nook Inc. wet suit and snorkel. You're spoilt for choice, really.

To get in the sea, run towards the water and press A when you get to the edge. You can also get in the sea by jumping off rocks or off the pier – again, just run towards the water and press A. Make sure you don't have any tools equipped before attempting to get in the water. Once you're in the water, keep tapping A to swim quickly.

CATCHING SEA CREATURES

'Sea creatures' is a broad term. You'll be able to collect lots of things that aren't technically creatures, such as seaweed and sea grapes. There are 40 new critters/items in total, and they each appear as a shadow on the ocean floor, with a stream of bubbles issuing up to the surface. The shadows are varying sizes and give an indication of the size of the creature or item. When you see a shadow, press Y to dive down and pick it up.

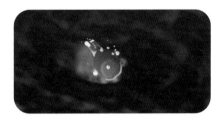

I got a mussel! It's been working out.

TIP

Tilt your camera to give you a top-down view – this will help you dive in just the right place to collect a sea creature.

SPECIAL GUEST APPEARANCE – PASCAL

Pascal is an otter with a penchant for scallops, and he's willing to trade you for them. You'll get one chance each day to see him, but he won't always appear the first time you catch a scallop, so be prepared to do quite a bit of diving. If you agree to give the scallop to Pascal, he'll reward you with a mermaid-themed recipe, a mermaid-themed item of clothing, or a pearl, which you'll need to craft the mermaid recipes.

Pascal

Hey, maaan, about that scallop of yours... can I have it?

DONATING SEA CREATURES TO THE MUSEUM

Check your Critterpedia for info about the sea creatures you've caught. Take any new discoveries to Blathers – he'll be delighted to rehome them in the museum aquarium, alongside the fish.

SELLING SEA CREATURES

I got a gigas giant clam! It's kind of a big deal.

Make sure you take duplicate sea creatures straight to Nook's Cranny, as some are quite valuable. Vampire squid, gigas giant clams, sea pigs, spider crabs and giant isopods are all worth 10,000 Bells or more.

MERMAID-THEMED ITEMS

Since you can only obtain the recipes for mermaid-themed items from Pascal, it'll take a while to collect them all. In addition to pearls, each recipe requires a different combination of shells. As you can see, the mermaid furniture goes very well with the shell furniture. And the mermaid fishy dress sets the whole scene off nicely.

MAKING BELLS

Want to become a Bellionaire? Of course you do – nobody's home development loans are getting any smaller, and you have big plans for your island. Follow these steps every day to make sure you have a constant influx of Bells.

1 SELL DUPLICATE FOSSILS

These can be worth up to 6,000 Bells each – sweep the island each day for fossils and take any duplicates to Timmy and Tommy at Nook's Cranny.

2 SELL UNWANTED ITEMS

Check your inventory and house storage for unwanted items. If you have a surplus of crafting materials like stones and clay, sell those too. Every little helps!

3 SELL FRUIT

Shake every fruit tree each day and sell everything you collect. Your native fruit will be worth 100 Bells apiece, but all other fruit is worth 500 Bells, except coconuts which are worth 250.

4
SELL SHELLS

Shells wash up on your beaches throughout the day, and can be retrieved from the ocean floor. They'll go for everything from 60 Bells (a cowrie) to 600 Bells (a summer shell).

5
SELL FISH

Catch as many fish as you can, and sell any duplicates. The larger the shadow size, the more the fish is likely to be worth.

Today's hot items (enquire inside!)
Hay bed
Shell bed

6
SELL HOT ITEMS FOR A FORTUNE

Check the board outside Nook's Cranny to find out what today's hot item is – Timmy and Tommy will pay you double what it's usually worth. It's always a craftable item, so this can be a really easy way to make Bells, provided you have the materials.

7

FIND THE MONEY ROCK

Hit all six rocks every day until you find the money rock. If you use the bracing trick, you can extract the maximum 15,800 Bells.

8

PLANT A MONEY TREE

Look for a glowing spot on the ground, dig with your shovel and you'll find 1,000 Bells. You can replant the Bells to create a money tree, which grows bags of Bells instead of fruit. If you have spare Bells in your pocket, replant 10,000 Bells instead of the 1,000 you dug up, and you'll get three bags of 10,000 Bells when the tree grows.

9

SHAKE THE TREES

Shake the trees and bells or random items may fall out. Of course, a wasps' nest may also fall out and then you'll get stung, so we suggest you do this whilst holding a net. That way, you'll be ready to pounce before they can sting you.

10 SHOOT DOWN YELLOW BALLOONS

Yellow balloons often contain Bells, so try to shoot them down if you see them. The most we've ever received from one balloon is 30,000 Bells.

Timmy

A Bell voucher!
Sure! How about if I offer you
3,000 Bells?

11 BUY BELL VOUCHERS

Head to the Nook Stop in the Town Hall to redeem your miles for Bell vouchers. Each voucher will cost you 500 Miles but can be sold for 3,000 Bells at Nook's Cranny. There's no limit to the number you can purchase each day – well, except the number of Miles you currently have.

12 TRACK DOWN CJ, FLICK OR LEIF

Remember that each of these characters will buy certain items from you for more than they're worth at Nook's Cranny. CJ loves fish, Flick is obsessed with bugs and Leif will happily buy all your weeds.

Leif

If you've got weeds, I'm buying!
20 Bells a clump.

THE STALK MARKET

This game really does reflect real life. There's even a version of the stock market called the stalk market – or Sow Joan's Stalk Market, to be precise. If you know what you're doing, playing the stalk market can make you a LOT of Bells.

SPECIAL GUEST APPEARANCE – DAISY MAE

Daisy Mae visits every Sunday, from 5am to 12pm. You can buy turnips from her in bunches of 10, so make sure you have some Bells ready. The price will be different each time she visits. The cheaper they are, the more money you can potentially make – it's always worth buying some if she's offering them for under 100 Bells per turnip. Make a note of how much the turnips cost so you can be sure to sell them at a profit.

Daisy Mae

I've got turnips a-plenty, fresh from Sow Joan's Stalk Market. Wanna buy 'em for 106 Bells each?

STORING TURNIPS

Turnips can't be stored in your home storage. You'll need to keep them in your inventory or drop them on the floor inside your house.

SELLING YOUR TURNIPS

You can sell your turnips at Nook's Cranny on every day except Sundays. Turnip value changes every morning and afternoon, so you'll be offered two different prices each day. Sometimes the price is random, sometimes there's a gradual decrease in value over the week, sometimes there's a small spike and, if you're very lucky, there might be a big spike. You should wait until Timmy and Tommy offer you a high amount before you sell, but you must sell your turnips by the following Saturday afternoon or they will rot. A good price is anything over 200 Bells, and very occasionally they might offer you 800 Bells per turnip.

ROTTEN TURNIPS

Although rotten turnips aren't worth anything, they will attract ants if you leave them on the ground. That's another bug you can add to the museum or sell at Nook's Cranny.

BALLOONS

In the world of Animal Crossing, presents literally fall from the sky. Isn't it marvellous? They come attached to balloons which can be shot down – all you need is a slingshot and a good aim.

FINDING BALLOONS

Balloons come in four colours: red, yellow, blue and green. They float across your island every few minutes. If you hear the sound of wind blowing, you'll know a balloon is nearby. Look up and keep following the sound until you spot the balloon. You may also see its shadow on the ground.

DID YOU KNOW? Once you've popped 300 balloons, the next balloon that appears will be a golden balloon. Pop this one and you'll be rewarded with the recipe for a golden slingshot.

SHOOTING BALLOONS DOWN

You can buy a slingshot from Nook's Cranny, or from Timmy at the Resident Services tent if the shop isn't set up yet. You can also buy the slingshot recipe from Nook's Cranny – that way, you can craft  your own slingshots in future. Stand directly below the balloon and use your catapult. If your aim is good, the balloon will pop and the present will fall to the ground. Make sure the balloon isn't floating over a lake or river when you shoot it – if it lands in water, you'll lose it. You'll need to shoot it down before it wafts out to sea and is gone for good, too.

PRESENTS

The present you get will be random, but some balloon colours seem to be more likely to contain certain items than others. This is still a matter of debate within the Animal Crossing community, but it looks like yellow balloons are more likely to contain Bells, blue balloons are more likely to contain crafting materials, red balloons are more likely to contain furniture and green balloons seem to contain a mix of items.

DID YOU KNOW? The first time you lose a balloon in water, you'll receive some Nook Miles. Well, at least that's something. Just don't let it happen again – you only get Miles the first time!

WISP

Fancy getting your hands on even more new items, as well as some Nook Miles? Then you'll want to track down Wisp. He only appears occasionally at night (well, he IS a ghost) so be sure to talk to him whenever you see him.

MEETING WISP

Wisp

**N-N-NOOOOOOOOOO!
A G-G-GHOOOOOOST!**

Wisp appears randomly – keep an eye out for him between the hours of 8pm and 4am. Here's the odd thing about Wisp: he's terrified of ghosts, despite the fact that he is one. When you approach him, he'll mistake you for an apparition and you'll give him such a scare that he'll lose his spirit. Most unfortunate.

DID YOU KNOW? You'll also earn Nook Miles for helping Wisp. So, even if you end up with a reward you're not thrilled about, at least your Miles total will have gone up.

> Wisp
> Um... I'm so sorry to ask, but... is there any chance you can collect the pieces of my spirit again?

> I caught a Wisp spirit piece! Finally, the third piece!

FINDING THE SPIRIT PIECES

Since you were the reason Wisp lost his spirit pieces, it's only right that you track them down and return them to him. There are five missing pieces in total – they look a little like raindrops and will be floating around nearby. Grab your net and get hunting!

YOUR REWARD

When you've caught all five spirit pieces, take them back to Wisp. He'll be so pleased that he'll offer you a reward. He'll give you the choice of something new or something expensive. Your instinct might be to go for the expensive item, but Wisp is a terrible judge of value, so you may end up with something that isn't worth much at all. It's much safer to choose something new – that way, you'll definitely get something you don't already have.

> Wisp
> I can get you something you don't have yet, or I can get you something expensive. So what's it going to be?

GULLIVER

Gulliver must be the unluckiest seagull in the world. Why does he wash up on our beaches so often? We may never know. But whatever's going on, the appearance of this bedraggled bird is an opportunity for you to get your hands on more rewards.

WAKING GULLIVER

When you spot Gulliver, he will be passed out on your beach. Rousing him may take some time – he's really out of it and all you'll get out of him at first is gibberish. Keep talking to him until he eventually gets to his feet. He'll try to call his crew on his communicator, before realising it's broken. This is where you come in – Gulliver wants you to help him locate his missing communicator parts.

Gulliver

Nnnn, don't wanna be flotsam... Can I be jetsam? It just sounds... more rugged... Zzz...

Gulliver

I'm begging you here! Will you look for my communicator parts? Please?

SEARCHING FOR THE COMMUNICATOR PARTS

The communicator parts will be buried along your beaches and appear as little jets of water coming out of the sand. They look exactly like the water jets produced by manilla clams, so be prepared to dig up several clams in addition to the missing hardware. Once you've found all five communicator parts, return them to Gulliver – make sure you do this on the same day that you meet him, otherwise they will rust and Gulliver will be gone.

I found a communicator part!

YOUR REWARD

As a reward for helping Gulliver, he'll send you a gift – it will arrive in the mail the following day. The items Gulliver hands out as rewards seem to be rare souvenirs from places around the world.

Gulliver

Be sure to check your mail in a few days. I'm gonna send you somethin' that'll knock your flippers off!

THE GOLDEN SHOVEL

If you help Gulliver 30 times, you'll be rewarded with the golden shovel recipe. Golden tools are the very best tools you can make in Animal Crossing, and carrying a golden tool tells the world that you're one of the most experienced Animal Crossing players out there.

GULLIVARRR

No – you didn't misread the title of this page. You're about to meet another seagull who looks suspiciously like Gulliver dressed as a pirate. He'll appear on your island about as often as Gulliver does, and he needs your help, too.

WAKING GULLIVARRR

Waking Gullivarrr is much like waking Gulliver – it'll take a few tries. Keep talking to him until he comes round. He'll try to get hold of his crew on his communicator, before realising that the communicator is missing. It'll be in the ocean somewhere nearby, and he'll ask you to retrieve it for him.

Gullivarrr

Arrr... Buccaneer? That's a bit out of me price range. Could I talk ye into a discount for both ears? Zzzz...

Gullivarrr

I'm begging ye, matey! Will ye help me find me communicator?!

SEARCHING FOR THE COMMUNICATOR

Put on your wet suit and get in the sea. The communicator will look like a stationery shadow on the ocean floor, with a stream of bubbles issuing from it. You'll probably catch several sea creatures before you find it, but keep at it and you'll soon find the missing piece of tech.

I found the communicator! Now to bring it to that pirate.

YOUR REWARD

Gullivarrr will be so grateful for the safe return of his precious communicator that he will send you a reward. It will arrive in the post the following day and it'll be something pirate-themed like this formidable pirate hat, a pirate treasure chest or a cannon.

ART

There's an impressive collection of famous art and statues available to buy in Animal Crossing. You can donate art to the museum, display it around the island or even in your home. But before you get too excited, be warned: all is not quite as it seems...

SPECIAL GUEST APPEARANCE – REDD

Redd has got to be Animal Crossing's shadiest character. He's an art dealer and he will sell you some genuinely valuable art... if you can spot it amongst all the fakes. He'll come to you the first time he visits your island, but from that point on, it's up to you to notice when his boat is in town. It'll dock at the very back of your island on what has come to be known within the Animal Crossing community as The Secret Beach.

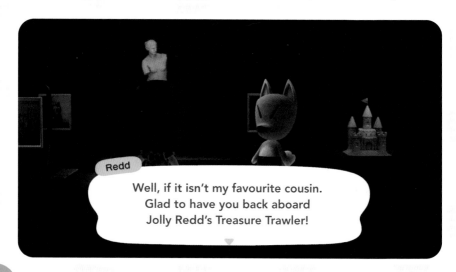

Redd

Well, if it isn't my favourite cousin. Glad to have you back aboard Jolly Redd's Treasure Trawler!

SPOTTING FAKE ART

Redd will usher you aboard his dimly-lit boat to peruse this week's collection. Perhaps he keeps the lights low to protect the artwork… more likely he's trying to stop customers getting too close a look at his wares. Enquire about a piece of art and Redd will offer you a price. If you know what you're looking for, you can take a closer look and make sure it's the real deal. If you do purchase any fakes, at least you'll know what to look out for next time! Spoiler alert: this one's fake.

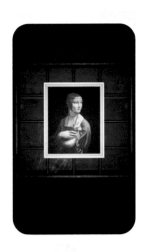

DONATING ART TO THE MUSEUM

Take your art to the museum to be appraised. Blathers will only accept genuine art, and will quickly tell you if you've brought him a fake.

MUSEUM ART GALLERY

If you play the game right, your museum art gallery will soon start to fill up. Blathers will make sure each piece is properly displayed, along with all the relevant information, so that everyone on the island can enjoy it.

ISLAND FASHION

One of the things we enjoy most about this game is getting to wear outfits we probably wouldn't be able to pull off in real life. And there's so much choice! From shopping at Able Sisters to creating custom clothing, here's our guide to looking your best while living your best island life.

ABLE SISTERS

Everyone knows that the Able Sisters' shop is THE place to buy fabulous outfits and accessories. Once Nook's Cranny is open, Mable will pop by to chat with Timmy and Tommy. She'll say hello to you, then she'll appear randomly on the plaza to sell a handful of wares. Purchase items from her a few times and it won't be long before she's asking you to help her find a suitable location for a permanent shop.

Mabel is the face of the store, but you'll see her sister, Sable, hard at work at the back. The first few times you try to talk to her she'll be too busy to speak to you, but if you talk to her every day, she'll eventually open up. Soon she'll be giving you gifts every time you speak to her – she has some brilliant custom designs which you can add to soft furnishings like beds and stalls.

Sable

I've just got a TON of work to get through. Thanks for understanding!

SPECIAL GUEST APPEARANCE – LABEL

Label

Why, hello, I'm Label, the fashion designer. I'm not sure if you've heard of me.

Mable and Sable have another sister called Label. Label works as a fashion designer, so she only visits the island occasionally. Make sure you chat to her when you spot her on the plaza – she'll ask you for help putting together outfits to fit certain themes, and she'll reward you with tailors tickets which you can redeem for items at Able Sisters.

SPECIAL GUEST APPEARANCE – KICKS

Kicks

Welcome, chum! Have a look. No rush, no rush at all.

Kicks the skunk has great taste in shoes and bags. He'll appear on the plaza every so often, with a collection of unique items for you to purchase – you won't find these accessories at the Able Sisters' shop.

OUTFIT IDEAS

Overwhelmed by the sartorial choices laid out before you? We've tried out hundreds of outfit combos and come up with some real winners. Here are our top picks to inspire you, whatever the occasion.

CEREMONY

On your way to a ceremony or other formal event? You can't go wrong with a blossoming kimono.

EXPLORER

Venturing out to a mystery island? Try the explorer look, complete with hat to protect you from the sun.

WORKOUT

If you're spending the day working on your physical health, a basketball tank, shorts and trainers are perfect.

IMP

Fancy giving your villagers something to talk about? The imp outfit is sure to attract comments. It comes in two delightful colours – purple and pink – and works for pretty much any occasion.

SUMMER SOLSTICE

To celebrate the Summer Solstice, try pairing the Summer Solstice Crown with the sleeveless silk dress. No need for shoes.

OLD SCHOOL

In the mood to relive the eighties or nineties? An old school jacket, acid wash jeans and high tops will strike the right vibe.

BEACH CASUAL

A sleeveless top, a pair of shorts, a sun hat and some sunglasses are perfect for a chilled day of beachcombing and fishing. Don't forget the flip flops!

PARTY

If one of your villagers is having a birthday, it's nice to make a bit of an effort. We recommend the comedian's outfit for maximum sparkle.

NAUTICAL

Spending the day gazing out to sea, or perhaps just helping Gulliver find his missing communicator parts? The sailor collar dress and sailor hat will do perfectly.

RAIN

You'll need a stylish raincoat and umbrella for those wet and dreary days. We love this colourful combo – the rainbow umbrella really cheers us up.

DUVET DAY

Sometimes you just need to spend the day lounging around in your favourite PJs. The DAL slippers will keep your feet cosy, too.

INCOGNITO

Whether you're having a bad hair day or hiding from the paparazzi, a long coat and the paper bag hat make for the perfect disguise. Trust us – nobody will have a clue who you are.

FRUIT-PICKING

Before you head to your orchard to do some fruit-picking, consider dressing up for the occasion. There are several fruit-themed outfits to choose from, so you're guaranteed to find one you like.

SPA DAY

Self-care is an important life skill. Why not invite some friends round to your home for an indulgent spa day? Don't forget the cucumber packs!

BIRTHDAY

On your birthday, you might want to wear something extra special. Choose whatever makes you happy, whether that's a wedding dress or a wrestler uniform.

WINTER SOLSTICE

Celebrate the winter solstice by wrapping up in cosy layers and a knit hat. The winter solstice jumper is guaranteed to make you feel festive.

STUDENT OF MAGIC

Do you dream of attending a famous school of witchcraft and wizardry? We don't blame you – we do, too! Now you can dress the part with the student gown and your favourite wand.

ASTRONAUT

If you're planning a long night of stargazing, consider dressing up in the astronaut outfit for dramatic flair – you'll feel out of this world!

CUSTOM CLOTHING DESIGNS

Once the Able Sisters' shop is open, you'll also be able to download complex custom clothing designs from all over the world, and share your own designs, too. Let's take a look at how custom clothing designs work.

THE CLOTHING RACK

The rack on the back wall is where the Able sisters display custom designs. If you want to download one of the designs from this rack, you'll need to save it over a blank design spot in your app, or delete one of your existing custom designs to make space.

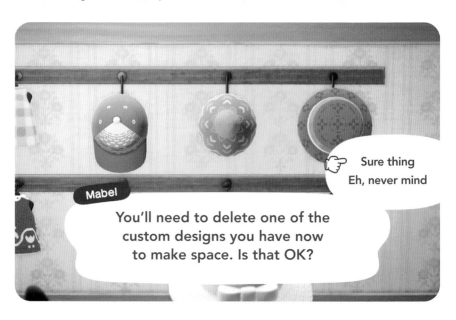

Sure thing
Eh, never mind

Mabel

You'll need to delete one of the custom designs you have now to make space. Is that OK?

THE CUSTOM DESIGNS PORTAL

The custom designs portal is on the back wall of Able Sisters. This is where you can share your own custom designs, and also download other people's designs from all over the world. You'll need to connect to the internet to view it. Once connected to the portal, you'll be given several search options. You can search by creator ID to view a designer's entire range, by design ID to view a single design, or by criteria to view designs by name or type. You can find creator IDs and design IDs on the internet – just search for 'best Animal Crossing clothing designs' or similar.

A world of creativity awaits here at the Custom Designs Portal!

UPLOADING YOUR DESIGNS

You can also design your own custom clothing using the custom design app – see pages 124–125 for more info on how to use the app. When you have a design you want to share, head to the clothing rack on the back wall. Choose a row, select an item, then select 'Display my work here' when Mabel asks you what you'd like to do. Your design will then be displayed for everyone to enjoy.

I want this design.
Display my work here.
Just browsing.

...So, what did you want to do?

MYSTERY ISLANDS

Mystery islands are a fantastic source of natural resources, as well as the place to be if you're looking to recruit a new villager. There are many different types, from islands covered with money rocks to islands crawling with tarantulas. Here's an overview of how to get there, as well as some of the most interesting mystery islands.

HOW TO GET TO A MYSTERY ISLAND

First you'll need a Nook Miles ticket – visit the Nook Stop and redeem 2,000 Miles for one ticket. Head to the airport and tell Dodo Airlines you want to fly, then tell them you want to use your Nook Miles Ticket.

Orville

So you wanna use your
Nook Miles Ticket? Roger!

Make sure you have plenty of free space in your inventory, as well as at least one of each tool – you're going to be collecting a lot of resources!

Mystery islands are bursting with life – there are flowers, bugs and fish to collect, as well as fossils to dig up. While you're there, make sure you strike every rock and shake every tree – on most islands, there will be an item hidden in the leaves of one of the trees. The resources on your own island aren't infinite and if you find yourself in desperate need of wood or iron, a visit to a mystery island will sort you out.

RESOURCES

Pop-up toaster

TRAVELLERS

Beau

Hey, nice to meet ya!
I'm Beau

If you currently have a vacant housing plot on your own island, you'll also meet another traveller on the mystery island. If you hit it off, you can invite them to move to your island – they always say yes. You'll get the option to invite them to live on your island the second time you talk to them.

MONEY ROCK ISLAND

8,000 Bells

This island has a small, central island with five money rocks. To get to the island you'll need to eat a piece of fruit, break the rock at the top of the outer island, and vault across. To get the maximum money from each rock, remove the stones first, as they're taking up valuable space. Don't forget to try the bracing trick!

FINNED FISH ISLAND

This is a great island for fish enthusiasts – it's home to finned fish only, including ocean sunfish, suckerfish and various sharks. You'll recognise it by the interesting mountain formation in the centre, which looks like a fin.

BAMBOO ISLAND

A favourite among mystery island-hoppers, this island is entirely covered with bamboo. You can use an axe to harvest the bamboo plants and dig up bamboo shoots from the holes next to the plants. The whole world of bamboo-themed recipes will be open to you once you've found this island.

CEDAR TREE ISLAND

This island is covered with cedar trees and coconut trees. What makes it particularly unusual is that it has no water features. It's a great place to chop wood and catch some tree-loving bugs.

TRASH ISLAND

This one's interesting, but for the wrong reasons. If you fish here, all you'll reel in is trash items like tyres, cans and stones. If you find yourself on trash island, stick to breaking rocks, chopping trees and catching bugs.

NON-NATIVE FRUIT ISLAND

This island will be packed with non-native fruit trees, i.e. different fruit to the one that grows naturally on your island. You'll want to grab as many pieces of fruit as you can carry.

WATERFALL ISLAND

This island is largely dominated by waterfalls and has three levels. It's a a really great place to catch rare fish that prefer clifftop locations.

HARDWOOD ISLAND

This is a great island to stumble upon if you're short on wood, since it's entirely covered with hardwood trees. Hope you remembered your axe!

DID YOU KNOW?

Rumour has it there's an island known as tarantula island, where only the bravest explorers dare go. If you stumble upon this island at night and you're skilled at catching arachnids, you can earn a large quantity of Bells – tarantulas sell for 8,000 Bells each.

HARV'S ISLAND

Harv's Island is the place to go if you want to take some awesome group shots of everyone on the island. It's essentially a house that's been turned into a photo studio. You can use it to create scenes and take as many photos as you need to until you finally get a shot where no one is blinking.

SPECIAL GUEST APPEARANCE – HARVEY

Harvey
Any time you want to visit, bud, just head to the airport and get aboard the Harv's Island Express.

Harvey will visit your island after the third villager moves in. He'll tell you all about his free photo studio and let you know that you're welcome to visit any time.

GETTING TO HARV'S ISLAND

Head to your airport, ask to fly, then ask to be taken to Harv's Island. Harv will be waiting to greet you when you arrive. You'll find him standing outside a log cabin – this is the photo studio, also known as Photopia.

DECORATING PHOTOPIA

Step inside Photopia and you'll discover it's a fully extended house. You'll have access to every home furnishing item you've ever unlocked through crafting or Nook Shopping, as well as any items you've ever found in trees or balloons. Open the inventory menu to begin adding items – you can import everything from furniture to floors and walls.

INVITING VILLAGERS

You can also bring your villagers into Photopia – just open the inventory menu and scroll along to the villager icon. Once you've dropped them into the room, you can move them around, dress them up in different outfits and make them perform reactions. If you have any Amiibo cards, you can use them to bring other characters in, too.

DID YOU KNOW? Next time you visit Harv's Island, Photopia will be exactly how you left it, with all the décor in place. If you want to clear a room, go into decorating mode and press Y to remove items.

VILLAGER POSTERS

Once you've taken some photos at Photopia, posters of the villagers you used will become available at the Nook Stop. You can purchase them and use them to decorate your home, or take them back to Harv's Island to use as part of a set.

VILLAGERS

The Animal Crossing villagers are a much-debated topic – opinion is divided about which ones are the best, and which are the worst. With 391 villagers to choose from, there's lots to discuss! Here's our guide to everything villager-related to help you get the Perfect Ten.

HOW TO FIND AND INVITE VILLAGERS

Once Nook's Cranny has opened, Tom will ask you to build three homes and some furnishings, to attract occupants. Any time you have a vacant housing plot, you can either wait for it to be filled by a random villager, or you can fill it yourself by meeting someone on a mystery island and inviting them to live on your island. If you prefer the latter option, you'd better be quick! Once your campsite is set up, you'll also be able to invite campers to live on the island permanently.

Whitney

That settles it, then! I'll move to Moonstone and start a new life there, snappy.

SETTING UP A CAMPSITE

Curt

Howdy! I'm just stakin' a claim for a bit, enjoyin' the campin' life. Be seein' you around, fuzzball!

Once your vacant housing plots have been filled, you'll need to set up a campsite before you can invite any other villagers to live on your island. Wait patiently and a camper will soon visit – you have to invite this camper to live on your island in order to progress any further. Now, Tom will offer you the option to sell additional plots of land until you have ten villager houses. Each plot will cost you 10,000 Bells, but you'll earn Nook Miles each time someone moves in.

PERSONALITY TYPES

There are several different personality types within the Animal Crossing world. A villager's personality dictates how they talk, what they wear, what they're interested in and how they get along with other villagers.

Lopez

No, no, no… It doesn't work like that. Pancakes are always breakfast, no matter when you eat them.

DID YOU KNOW?

It takes a while for villagers to really warm up to you, so keep chatting to them every day. At first they may not have much to say, but soon they'll be inventing nicknames for you, sending you letters and asking for favours.

Jock villagers are obsessed with health and exercise – expect a lot of chat about protein shakes, patrol jogs and lifting weights. Their idea of a compliment is to tell you you're 'looking built'. They like to spend time out and about on the island rather than sitting at home – you'll often spot them lifting weights and stretching. Jocks don't get along with snooty and lazy villagers and often end up in arguments with them. You always get a jock as one of your starting villagers.

Dom

It's a great day for some cross-training!

Scoot

MUSCLE MADNESS!

Bam

This weather REALLY gets the muscles glistenin', kablang!

Roald

Plus, I scouted out a great spot for my place. It's central to at least 10 jogging routes that I know of!

SISTERLY VILLAGERS

Sisterly villagers, also called uchi villagers, are generally kind and caring and try to look after you – they're the ones who will offer you medicine if you've been stung by wasps. When they're out and about, you'll often spot them singing or dancing. Cranky and snooty villagers find them annoying. They can be quite selfish, and sometimes even a little blunt. Everyone gets one sisterly villager as a starter villager.

Cherry

What is UP, superstar!

Agnes

Gotta stop and smell the flowers
now and then, y'know? Running
around everywhere'll wear you out!

LAZY VILLAGERS

Lazy villagers are the opposite of jocks in many ways. They love snacking and resting and are very laid-back and easy-going. They are generally friendly to other villagers and seem to be very interested in the island and its wildlife – particularly bugs. Jock villagers find lazy villagers difficult to get along with, and snooty villagers tend to look down on them. Lazy villagers get on well with cranky villagers as they both prefer the quiet, slow life.

Cole

Morniiing. A super yummy smell woke me up earlier than usual!

Zucker

Moonstone is the perfect size. Too big to see across, but too small for a sea monster to attack!

Boomer

If I get my clothes dirty on rainy days, I just go outside and jump in puddles for an hour or two.

Beau

I like watering flowers. It's nice to take care of something and see it grow.

PEPPY VILLAGERS

You can't miss the peppy villagers – they're excitable, high-energy and usually in a very good mood. They're friendly towards everyone and spend a lot of time outdoors, spreading joy and smiles wherever they go. Many peppy villagers dream of being pop stars and will tell you all about their plans. Snooty and cranky villagers can be quite negative towards peppy villagers. Although peppy villagers are generally very happy, they will be rude to you if you're rude to them.

Ketchup

OHMIGOSH! Not to get, you know, off topic, but... if I had a castle, that'd make me the princess.

Flora

If I just spend money on everything, my whole eventual-pop-star fortune will be gone in no time!

Sprinkle

HIHOWAREYOUI'MPRETTYGOOD I'MGOINGFORAWALKTOWORK OFFTHISCOFFEEBUZZ'KBYE!

Pompom

Sometimes, when I can't wake up in the morning, I run in circles and scream really loud for a few minutes!

SNOOTY VILLAGERS

Snooty villagers have an air of superiority about them. They dress well and decorate their homes with luxurious items. Although they are well spoken, they can also be rude and sarcastic. Building up a friendship with a snooty villager usually encourages them to warm up. They find lazy villagers impossible to understand, but find jocks equally as perplexing – to them, fashion is everything. Snooty villagers don't get on well with normal villagers or sisterly villagers, but get along fine with cranky and smug villagers.

Freya

I hope you have something exciting planned for today. It can be quite invigorating to change your routine!

Mint

The plaza is the public face of the island, after all, so of course we want it to look its best!

Whitney

One mustn't be afraid of a bit of wet weather. Just think of the rain as an excuse to accessorise, snappy!

Olivia

Ooh, that Raymond! Get a life! Have your own interests! Is that really so hard to do?!

SMUG VILLAGERS

Smug villagers have impeccable manners and usually get along well with other villagers. They are generally upbeat and spend a lot of time outdoors. They can be quite conceited, however, and have been known to blow their own horns. They usually get on well with lazy, peppy and normal villagers. They can struggle to get along with jocks, sisterly villagers and cranky villagers.

Pietro

Yo! You wanna chat?
I don't blame you, Kablam!

Lopez

Ah, another sunny, beautiful day
in paradise. SO glad I decided to
live the island life...

Raymond

Don't be shy, Eidothean.
I see you eyeing my dashing, yet
seasonally appropriate attire.

Marshal

I guess you must have splurged
for the all-access pass, huh?
Marshal Unlimited!

CRANKY VILLAGERS

Cranky villagers are quite selfish, easy to annoy and likely to get into arguments with other villagers. When you first meet them, they may seem grumpy and rude, but the more you get to know them, the more they warm up. They tend to get on well with snooty villagers and jocks, but find peppy, sisterly and smug villagers very difficult. If you neglect them, they will quickly let you know.

Grizzly

This is really janglin' up my nerves...
Tickin' me off somethin'
fierce too!

Apollo

Well, glad to know we're still
neighbourly! Stop by again
soon, alright?

Dobie

Oh, hey there, Eidothean.
You know what burns
my beans?

Gaston

Let's try to beat this
dadburn heat!

NORMAL VILLAGERS

Normal villagers are pleasant with everyone and difficult to upset. They tend to be neutral on many topics and always try to be kind. They get on well with smug and lazy villagers, but find cranky villagers difficult. They like cleaning and cooking and will often talk to you about food.

Today's already fun, doyoing!

They say you shouldn't start your day without a plan, but they also say plans are a fool's errand, so...

I thought maybe you could use some pixel shades.

I try to be a good listener. You can talk to me anytime, blurp.

BEING A GOOD FRIEND

Since Animal Crossing is a game all about community and friendship, you'll want to make sure you're being the very best friend you can possibly be. Don't worry – we've got you covered. Here's everything you need to know about island friendship.

FRIENDSHIP LEVELS

Your friendship level with each villager is constantly increasing or decreasing based on how many positive interactions you have with them. And why would you want to improve your friendship levels, you ask? Because if you achieve best friend status with a villager, they'll reward you with a framed photo of themselves – a rare and precious item you won't find anywhere else.

LEVEL 1

FRIEND (0–29 points)

When a villager first moves to your island, you'll be level 1 friends.

Lots of clouds in the sky today.
They look like cotton candy…
Gotta find a ladder so I can bite 'em!

LEVEL 2

FRIEND (30–59 points)

After talking to new villagers a couple of times, you'll hit level 2. Level 2 friends can exchange gifts.

LEVEL 3

GOOD FRIEND (60–99 points)

Once you've exchanged a few gifts, you'll hit level 3, at which point the villager is able to sell items to you.

LEVEL 4

GOOD FRIEND (100–149 points)

When you hit level 4, you'll be able to change your villager's catchphrase.

Be honest… What do you think of my catchphrase?

LEVEL 5

BEST FRIEND (150–199 points)

Congratulations – you've made it to best friend status! At level 5, there's a chance the villager might give you a framed photo of themselves. You can also change their greeting.

LEVEL 6

BEST FRIEND (200–255 points)

It doesn't get any better than this – at level 6, villagers will be able to trade furniture with you.

HOW TO INCREASE YOUR FRIENDSHIP LEVEL

Keen to reach level 6 friendship with someone special?
Follow these steps and you'll be best buds in no time.

1 **TALK TO VILLAGERS EVERY DAY**

Make sure you talk to your villagers every day, so they know you care about them. When a villager has a thought bubble over their head, they will either have a gift for you, a favour to ask or want to talk to you about something more serious. Always stop and talk to them when they're in this thoughtful state.

2 **AGREE TO VILLAGERS' REQUESTS**

Marina

Would you consider buying my things? I really want to read that book, bloop!

If a villager asks you to do something – find them a specific bug, play a game with them, buy a hideous outfit from them for an over-inflated price – always say yes. You'll earn friendship points and keep them happy.

3

CATCH VILLAGERS' FLEAS

Even the cleanest, most respectable villagers occasionally get fleas. If they tell you they're feeling itchy, take a very close look at them and see if you can spot a flea hopping around. Catch it with your net and they will be eternally grateful.

Whitney

Oh, mercy! I had fleas?! I didn't even realise... I thought I was so fresh and clean and... flealess.

Sprinkle

Ohmigosh! Is this... a globe?

4

GIVE GIFTS

Try to give your villagers gifts once a day. You'll earn bonus points if the gift caters to their personality, and even more bonus points if it's wrapped. Often, you'll receive a gift in return.

SEND NOTES

You can send notes to your villagers from the airport. If you attach a gift, you'll get even more friendship points.

Hmm... They have a card stand here. Looks like I can send a message on a card for 200 Bells.

6 ## REMEMBER VILLAGERS' BIRTHDAYS

Make sure you pop by villagers' homes on their birthday – there'll be a party going on and they'll really appreciate the effort you made. You'll earn even more points if you take a wrapped present.

7

VISIT SICK VILLAGERS

If you notice one of your villagers hasn't been out and about, they might be sick. Make an effort to visit them at home and take some medicine – this will earn you major friendship points.

Fauna

You p-probably went out of your w-way to pick this up.

8

RETURN LOST ITEMS

Sometimes you'll find a lost item on the ground. Find a villager and ask if it's theirs – if it isn't, they'll usually know whose it is. Returning it will earn you more friendship points.

Sprinkle

Whoa, I totes cannot believe you found this! I thought this comic was lost forever!

DID YOU KNOW? If you accidentally push a villager or hit them with a net, you'll lose friendship points. Be very careful where you walk and what you swipe at!

HOW TO GET RID OF UNWANTED VILLAGERS

Let's be honest: sometimes you just don't gel well with a certain villager. Maybe they've creeped you out, or annoyed you to the point that you're desperate to get rid of them. Don't feel bad – it happens to everyone. If you're absolutely sure you want to vote someone off the island, here's how it's done.

DID YOU KNOW?

Villagers tend to start talking about leaving after they've been on your island for a while. But that doesn't mean you have to let them! If you want them to stay, tell them.

STRATEGY 1: THE COLD SHOULDER

This phase is all about ignoring the villager. Don't speak to them for several days, but make sure you continue to speak to everyone else. After a few days, you should see the villager wandering around with a thought bubble over their head. Now's the time to go and talk to them – they'll likely tell you they're thinking of moving away. You'll be given two response options – choose the option that encourages them to move away, and that'll be that.

Chops

Well, there it is. I guess I'm leaving! Thanks for everything.

STRATEGY 2: INVITE A CAMPER USING AN AMIIBO CARD

You'll need to get hold of an Amiibo card for a villager you'd like to live on your island, then head to the Nook Stop and invite them to your campsite. When they visit, they'll ask you to craft something for them. You'll need to invite the camper three times, on three separate days, and fulfil any crafting requests before you can invite them to move to your island. At this point, you will be asked to choose which of the existing villagers should move out. Even better, your new villager will have the difficult conversation for you.

Ketchup

I asked Grizzly like you told me to... and he agreed!

STRATEGY 3: TAKE A CHANCE ON A RANDOM CAMPER

This strategy works much the same way as the Amiibo card strategy, but the camper may decline your offer to move to the island. The first time a camper visits, there's a 10% chance they will say yes to your invitation. If you see the same camper again and invite them to move to the island, the chance of them saying yes increases to 50%. Some campers will even make you play a game to determine whether they will move in.

Graham

Let's play a quick card game. If you win, I'll move here. If I win, I won't.

CELESTIAL EVENTS

If you look up on clear nights, you may see some exciting things happening in the sky above your island. Shooting stars and meteor showers bring the opportunity to collect magical star fragments, which can be used to craft a wand and several zodiac-themed items.

SPECIAL GUEST APPEARANCE – CELESTE

Celeste is one of our absolute favourite visitors. She's Blathers' sister, and has a keen interest in astronomy, which means she's also the bringer of zodiac-themed recipes. She appears after 7pm on nights when shooting stars will be seen. If you spot her, make sure to do a bit of stargazing before you go to bed.

Celeste

Its not scientific, but I just know if you make your wish before the star disappears, it will be granted!

METEOR SHOWERS AND SHOOTING STARS

If there's going to be a meteor shower, Isabelle will tell you in the morning briefing. Whereas shooting stars come in handfuls of only a few per night, meteor showers are special events in which hundreds of shooting stars appear.

WISHING ON A STAR

To wish on a star, you'll need to wait until after 7pm, and the sky will need to be clear. Find a spot where you have an unobstructed view of the sky and look up. Put away the tool you're carrying so that your hands are empty. Wait patiently, and after a while you'll hear a musical sound and a star will shoot across the sky. While looking up at the star, press A to make a wish. Keep wishing on stars until you've made 20 wishes – you'll get one star fragment per wish, but you can never get more than 20 star fragments in total.

TIP

Invite friends to your island on shooting star or meteor shower nights, and they'll be able to wish on stars, too. In addition to your own limit of 20 star fragments, you'll get one star fragment for each wish your friend makes – they'll find star fragments on their island the next day as well.

STAR FRAGMENTS

The morning after you've wished on some stars, you'll find several star fragments have washed up on your beaches overnight – some will be regular star fragments, some will be large star fragments and some will be zodiac star fragments. The zodiac star fragment will correspond to the current zodiac sign that's in the sun. Regular star fragments are the most common, and you may only get one large star fragment or zodiac fragment. Keep checking your beach throughout the day, as they wash up in waves – there can only be 10 star fragments on your beaches at any one time.

Star fragment

Large star fragment

Gemini fragment

DID YOU KNOW? The colour of the zodiac-themed star fragments corresponds to the birthstone for that month.

ZODIAC-THEMED ITEMS

Once you've collected some star fragments and been gifted some celestial-themed recipes by Celeste, you can start crafting zodiac-themed items. The first recipe she'll give you is for a wand – more about that on the next page – then she'll start giving you zodiac-themed recipes corresponding to the zodiac fragments that are currently washing up on your beaches.

OTHER CELESTIAL ITEMS

In addition to recipes for wands and zodiac-themed items, Celeste is the keeper of recipes for all things celestial. Keep talking to her each time she visits and you'll soon have recipes for celestial objects, walls and floors and even fashion items.

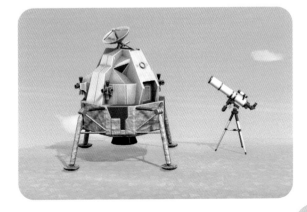

WANDS

Wands are rare, magical items which allow you to transform your appearance in an instant. Although they all do the same thing, there are lots of different wands to collect. They're an essential tool for fashion-conscious islanders.

STAR WAND

The first time you talk to Celeste, she'll give you a recipe for a star wand. This will be the beginning of your obsession with wand outfits.

REGISTERING OUTFITS TO WANDS

Once you have a wand, you can start to register outfits. You can have up to eight wand outfits. Just go to a closet and choose 'edit wand outfits'. From here, you can create an outfit for each of the eight wand slots, using clothes and accessories you own.

USING WANDS

When you want to transform and put on one of your wand outfits, just hold your wand and press A. You can scroll through all eight outfits and choose the one you want. When you want to return to normal, just hold your wand again, press A and remove the outfit.

EXPANDING YOUR WAND COLLECTION

There are lots of wands for you to collect. Celeste has many recipes, but others can be obtained by taking part in events like Bug Offs, Fishing Tourneys and Wedding Season.

DID YOU KNOW? You can't use the Able Sisters' fitting room when under the effect of a transformation wand.

VISITOR ETIQUETTE

When you visit other people's islands, it's important to behave well. Otherwise, you won't get invited back! Here are our top tips for being the perfect guest whilst also making the most of your visit.

1 DO BRING A GIFT

Bring a gift to say thank you for the host's hospitality. You could check in with them before their visit to see if there's anything in particular they're looking for.

2 DON'T TAKE ANY ITEMS WITHOUT ASKING

If you want to take some fruit or dig up a flower, ask permission first. If you get the go-ahead, take only what you need – don't be greedy.

3 DO CATCH A FEW BUGS AND FISH

Bugs and fish are generally considered fair game when you visit another island. If you catch something rare or valuable, consider giving it back to your host.

4 DO CHECK OUT THEIR SHOPS

Just make sure you don't help yourself to any limited items in Nook's Cranny without asking your host if they want them.

5

DON'T TRAMPLE THE FLOWERS

Running around a strange new island can be loads of fun – just don't run through the flowers, or you'll knock the petals off.

7

DO SELL YOUR ITEMS AT NOOK'S CRANNY

Feel free to offload some unwanted items at Nook's Cranny so you can make space in your inventory. This includes turnips, if the price is right.

6 DO USE YOUR REACTIONS

Typing properly-worded messages to your friends in the chat function can take ages, so it's best to stick to reactions where possible. If you really want to chat, stick to abbreviations like TYSM (thank you so much).

8 DON'T ABUSE YOUR BEST FRIEND PRIVILEGES

Being best friends with someone means you can use your axe and shovel on their island. But don't abuse this right, or you'll likely find yourself off the list.

9 DON'T GET MISCHIEVOUS

Never do anything deliberately annoying like hitting your friend with a net or monopolising the Able Sisters' changing room for half an hour.

THE HAPPY HOME ACADEMY

All homeowners are automatically registered with the Happy Home Academy. The HHA evaluates your home each Sunday at 5am. They also send you the occasional bit of helpful advice and reward you with items if they like what they see.

HHA RANKINGS

The HHA will award your home one of three rankings: B, A or S. B is the lowest and S is the highest. You'll get rewards at each stage, which include pennants and trophies.

THE S RANKING

To earn maximum points and be awarded the coveted S ranking, you'll need to create a home that meets the requirements for as many of the following criteria as possible.

1 KEEP YOUR HOME TIDY

That means no dropped recipes and items. If you don't log in to the game for a month, cockroaches will appear in your home. Obviously this is a major no-no for the HHA.

2 INCLUDE THE ESSENTIAL FURNITURE ITEMS

Make sure you have a bed, a chair, a table and a wardrobe – these are considered essential items for any home.

3 PUT FURNITURE IN EVERY ROOM

The HHA won't be impressed by an empty room, no matter how magnificent your other rooms look. Make sure each room has a purpose and some furniture.

4 INCLUDE A VARIETY OF FURNITURE SETS

Furniture comes in sets, like the mermaid set, the antique set and the ironwood set. Including items from a wide variety of sets will get you more points.

DID YOU KNOW? When you upgrade your house, the HHA will send you a gift to help you celebrate.

5 PLACE ITEMS FROM THE SAME FURNITURE SET IN THE SAME ROOM

Try to keep furniture sets together, and stick to one or two furniture sets per room. If you display a complete set within one room, you'll get even more points.

6 PICK A COLOUR SCHEME FOR EACH ROOM

Sticking to an obvious colour scheme for each room is a great way to increase your HHA score and make your interior décor look well thought out.

TIP

In addition to visiting Nook's Cranny every day in search of homewares, don't forget to check out Nook Shopping at the Nook Stop. You can order a maximum of five items per day, and they stock special goods and seasonal items, as well as everything you've already bought.

7 INCORPORATE FENG SHUI

Feng shui is kind of a big deal in Animal Crossing and will earn you more points. All you need to do is place one red item on the right side of a room, one yellow item on the left, one green at the bottom and leave some space clear in the centre.

8 INCLUDE LUCKY ITEMS

Certain items, like the ring, the golden candlestick, the crescent moon chair and the lucky gold cat, are considered to be lucky items. Placing them around your home will increase the number of points you are awarded.

LOSING POINTS

The HHA will dock points if you have non-furniture items like recipes dropped on the floor, furniture facing the walls or, horror of all horrors, a cockroach problem. Remember that cockroaches will appear if you don't log into the game for a month.

HOME INTERIOR INSPIRATION

Once you've expanded your home, you can have loads of fun decorating. The Animal Crossing community is incredibly creative and and they've turned home décor into an art form. Here are some fun room ideas to get you started.

SPECIAL GUEST APPEARANCE – SAHARAH

Saharah the camel is the person to see if you're looking for unique rugs, walls and floors – she'll visit your island every so often to peddle her wares. Buying a rug from Saharah will earn you Saharah tickets – get five of these and you can trade them for another rug, wall or floor.

Saharah

Hello. You are calling me Saharah, for it is the name I have carried for as long as I have carried these rugs.

AQUARIUM BATHROOM

Turn your bathroom into an atmospheric aquarium with the underwater wall, underwater flooring and an entire wall full of aquatic creatures displayed in tanks.

CELESTIAL BEDROOM

What better theme for a bedroom than the night sky? Pair the starry wall with the galaxy floor and throw in lots of zodiac-themed items.

FANCY FOYER

This is the first room visitors will see, so make it impressive! Think high contrast colours, antique furniture, musical instruments and a statement wall.

RETRO KITCHEN

Pair your favourite floral wallpaper with a retro floor and some bright kitchen accessories for a delightfully old-fashioned vibe.

UNDER THE SEA BEDROOM

Have fun combining the mermaid set and the shell set to create the perfect under the sea bedroom. You can get this marine pop wallpaper as a reward for competing in the fishing tourney.

PLANT ROOM

How many plants can you fit in one room? Turns out it's quite a few. We love the arched window wall and a stone floor for that conservatory feel, plus a combination of ironwood and rattan furniture.

ARCADE ROOM

The gamer in you will love this idea – it works best in a dark basement. Try the fireworks wallpaper with plenty of arcade games, neon lights and perhaps a jukebox.

MUSIC ROOM

In the mood to jam with your friends? You can set up your very own music room so you can make all your rock star fantasies come true. Don't forget to stick a rug under the drumkit to make it look realistic.

SECRET LABORATORY

This is another great themed room to try out in your basement. You can come down here to invent incredible inventions and concoct special concoctions. Any items with a remotely scientific theme will work, and if they're leaking luminous fluid, so much the better.

SEWING ROOM

In the real world, very few people can afford to dedicate an entire room to sewing. But this is Animal Crossing, where anything is possible. Here, we've paired a variety of antique furnishings with an elaborate kimono stand and some colour-coordinated outfits.

WITCHY ROOM

Find a dark corner of your house and furnish it with items made from stone and wood. We've added plenty of moss balls, flowers and plants, as well as some cobwebs. Nobody in the Animal Crossing community seems to know what a kettle bathtub is for, but we're using ours as a cauldron.

CUSTOM DESIGNS

Animal Crossing is an incredibly creative game, and no doubt you'll want to try your hand at designing some awesome patterns. That's where the Custom Designs app comes in – it gives you the ability to create your own designs for everything from homewares and paths to clothing.

DID YOU KNOW?

The Pro Designs app is an add-on to the Custom Designs app – you can get it in exchange for 800 Nook Miles when you visit the Nook Stop.

CUSTOM DESIGNS TAB

Open the custom designs tab and you'll see a selection of pre-loaded designs and patterns ready for you to use. These can be worn, displayed on mannequins, displayed as paintings or displayed on the ground. They can also be used to create paths if you select them in your Island Designer app. When you're feeling creative, you can select one of the blank design squares and design your own pattern – just choose 'change design'.

CUSTOM DESIGN TOOLS

These may look scary at first, but they're easy to use once you get the hang of them. First, choose your tool by pressing X. You can use the pen tool for small details, the fill tool to cover the entire design in a single colour, and various shaped tools to create circles, hearts, stars and more. Once you've selected the tool you want to use, find the right colour by using L and R to scroll through the options. When you're happy with your design, press + to confirm the name and save it to your app.

PRO DESIGNS TAB

The Pro Designs tab is designed to create clothing. You'll find several designs pre-loaded and lots of spaces for you to create your own. You'll be asked to choose a garment of clothing to design before you can get creative. You will then be given access to the design tools again so you can create your sartorial masterpiece.

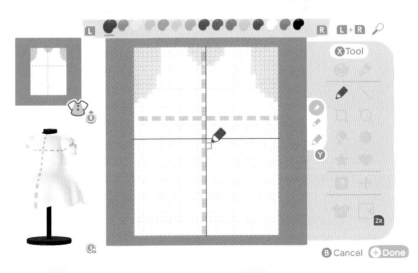

DECORATING YOUR ISLAND – THE BASICS

Decorating your island gives you a chance to show off your creative side, as well as increase your island's rating. Let's take a look at some sure-fire ways to get that island rating up to three stars so you can unlock the terraforming app and get a very special visitor.

PLANT FLOWERS

This is a very easy way to add splashes of colour to your island as well as to increase your island rating. Plant as many varieties as possible – fill every corner, and don't forget to have fun breeding hybrid colours.

PLANT TREES

Planting a variety of trees across your island is a great way to increase your rating, but you can also have too much of a good thing. Don't plant so many that there's no room to place other objects – Isabelle will let you know if you've gone too far.

BUILD FENCES

Placing fencing around your island will also help you to achieve 3-star status. You can use fences to encircle your buildings or to divide areas into different sections.

PLACE FURNITURE OUTSIDE

You can have lots of fun with this one. Choose pieces you think will work well outside, and position them all over your island. Obvious choices include chairs, tables and benches, but think outside the box, too. This is a good time to start thinking about what you'd like your overall island aesthetic to be.

BUILD BRIDGES

Your villagers need a way to cross the water, and you'll get fed up using your vaulting pole soon enough. You can have a maximum of eight bridges on your island – go and speak to Tom Nook and he'll show you the catalogue.

CREATE INCLINES

Your villagers also need a way to scale your island's cliffs, so create some well-placed inclines as soon as you can. Tom is the person to see about these, too. As with bridges, you can only have eight, so choose carefully.

DID YOU KNOW? To check on your current island evaluation, go and see Isabelle in the Town Hall and choose the 'let's talk island evals' option. She'll give you some feedback from an anonymous person as well as some tips on how to increase your rating.

MAKE YOURSELF A GARDEN

Create a small space where you can relax after a busy day of island development. You can do this for your villagers, too. There are lots of garden-themed items you can incorporate, and you can use fencing to create a boundary if you aren't on a cliff.

SPECIAL GUEST APPEARANCE – K K SLIDER

Once your island achieves a 3-star rating, the fun can really begin. K K Slider will make Tom Nook's dreams come true and finally agree to play a gig on the island! He'll visit every Sunday after that, to perform more gigs, and will also pop in to play a special gig on your birthday. What a great guy – no wonder Tom was so keen to get him to visit.

TERRAFORMING IDEAS

Once you've unlocked the Island Designer app, you can really start to make the island your own. You can create and demolish cliffs and water features and also create paths. Here are some terraforming ideas to get you started.

DID YOU KNOW? You can purchase different permits for your Island Designer App at the Nook Stop, including different path designs.

HEART LAKE

This is a very popular feature with the Animal Crossing community, because it's fun and easy to create. Just use your waterscaping tool to create two channels at 90 degrees to each other, then round off the edges to give the appearance of a heart.

DOUBLE WATERFALL

This is another easy island feature that's sure to turn heads. Find or create a spot where there are three separate levels, then use your waterscaping tool to create a waterfall ending in a lake or a river at the bottom.

STEPPING STONES

Stepping stones look great, and can come in handy if you've used up your quota of bridges. Just use your waterscaping tool to create squares of land in the middle of any large body of water.

ISLAND WITHIN AN ISLAND

This is exactly what it sounds like – a small island surrounded by water, in the middle of your island. You can construct bridges so you can easily get back and forth, or create stepping stones across the river. If you need a little peace and quiet, you could move your house here and get rid of the bridges, so the only way to access it is using a vaulting pole.

WATERFALL WALL

This dramatic backdrop works well behind lots of features, from shops and houses to flower fields. It's achieved by using your cliff construction tool to create two drops in quick succession, then adding water with your waterscaping tool. As an added bonus, the sound of the rushing water is very relaxing.

SECRET GARDEN

Accessible via a sneaky side entrance, this secret garden is the perfect spot to take a quiet moment for yourself. Just dig a narrow tunnel into the side of one of your cliffs, and hollow out an area inside, then decorate it using your favourite flowers. Don't forget to include somewhere to sit.

INFINITY POOL

Always dreamed of living the millionaire lifestyle? Well, now you can enjoy your own private infinity pool. Head to the top of a cliff and use your waterscaping tool to create a pool that goes to the very back edge. The view at sunrise and sunset will be breathtaking.

WATERFALL WALKWAY

This stunning island feature is sure to get visitors talking. The waterfalls are created in the same way as the waterfall wall, but they run from the front to the back of your island, forming a dramatic path to a secluded area, a shop or even your house.

MAZE

Let's have a little fun, shall we? This maze is a great feature to enjoy with island visitors. Get creative with your cliff construction tool and make an intricate labyrinth of passages that are guaranteed to get you truly lost. You could drop a present at the centre of the maze for anyone skilled enough to make it that far.

FLOODED ISLAND

If you like playing around with the waterscaping tool, you'll love creating a flooded island. More water than land, a flooded island is made up of lots of interconnected rivers, with small islands dotted in between. You could try putting each building on a different island and getting creative with stepping stones to help you move between them.

CRESCENT MOON LAKE

Celestial objects are very important in Animal Crossing, so why not celebrate that by making a crescent moon lake? It can be a little tricky to get the shape right, but the one we made should help you. If you decorate it with star fragments it'll look lovely at night.

ISLAND FEATURE IDEAS

With an inventory full of decorative items and the terraforming app on your Nook Phone, you're ready to make this island your own. Before we dive into entire island aesthetics, let's take a look at some ideas for smaller features.

SPECIAL GUEST APPEARANCE – LUNA

Anyone with a Nintendo Switch online membership can meet Luna by sleeping in a bed. She'll offer you the chance to visit other people's islands for inspiration. You'll need a dream address for the island you want to visit – you can find these online by searching for 'Animal Crossing dream address'.

Luna

Once within the dream of another, it will be as though you have actually set foot on their island.

MUSEUM ENTRANCE

You can make your museum entrance look even more impressive by decorating it with fossils. If you're short on space you can stick to smaller fossils like ammonites, but a T-rex skeleton will leave visitors in no doubt as to what's inside.

CAMPSITE

Develop the area around your campsite to make it look like it's in the middle of a forest. Plant some cedar trees, add weeds and place some log furniture and campware until you're happy with the effect.

PICNIC AREA

Who doesn't love a picnic? Get creative with your Custom Design app and make a path that resembles your favourite picnic blanket, then place some of your favourite picnic items on top. You could include something to eat, something to read and perhaps something to listen to, as well.

CAFÉ

Find a quiet corner to create a cute café. You can use a custom stall and espresso maker to make a counter, then place some iron garden furniture so visitors can take a seat while they get their caffeine fix. If you can, position it next to a pretty feature like a waterfall.

SPIRAL GARDEN

This is a simple design that looks fantastic when completed. We've used a combination of hedges, shrubs and flowers to give the borders some variety, and positioned an iron bench in the centre so residents can sit and watch the butterflies flutter by.

SPA

Everyone on the island can take time to unwind in this relaxing spa. Tatami beds and cypress bathtubs perfectly complement the terracotta tile floor, giving a relaxed, natural feel.

ORCHARD

This is another popular island feature within the Animal Crossing community. An orchard is attractive and practical – it provides you with lots of fruit, which you can sell or craft into fruit-themed items, as well as a source of wood. You'll also attract lots of tree-loving bugs.

CHILDREN'S PLAYGROUND

The perfect build for the young at heart, this children's playground will help to brighten up your island and remind everyone to have some fun once in a while. The teacup ride is an obvious choice, along with a sandbox and a springy ride-on.

GRAVEYARD

Put your western-style stones to good use by creating a creepy graveyard – perhaps dedicated to the villagers who've left your island. Plant black flowers, weeds and trees around the stones, and use the iron and stone fence to create a perimeter. If you have a flair for the dramatic, you could also add a skeleton or two.

ZEN GARDEN

A truly peaceful spot, the zen garden is the perfect retreat for people who need to slow down. Plant some shrubs and bamboo and add a few zen details like cushions and lanterns. Your villagers will soon be flocking here to focus on their breathwork.

GOLF COURSE

Anyone for a round of golf? This golf course is very simple to put together. Leave the grass untouched for the fairway, but add weeds, shrubs, trees and other details to the rough along the edges. The outdoor bath makes for an interesting water feature.

SWIMMING POOL

If you love the beach life then why not create a swimming pool area near to the ocean? Use your terraforming app to create a sandy patch, add a pool and some beach-themed items, and you're all set.

RESTAURANT

Who doesn't love eating al fresco? There are lots of ways to theme an outdoor restaurant – classic elegance, sushi or even a good old-fashioned American diner. Here we've created a fancy clifftop restaurant, complete with live music.

FLOWER MARKET

Customise some stalls and set up a flower market that's bursting with colourful blooms. The garden wagon can be customised to complement your stalls, and you can even throw in a wedding flower stand or two.

FARM

You can't actually grow crops in Animal Crossing, but don't let that stop you creating a farm. Place weeds or turnips on rows of dirt path and surround them with every farm-related item you can get your hands on.

ISLAND AESTHETICS

What kind of island do you want to create? If you're looking for a little inspiration, the next few pages are just what you need. We've gathered together some of our favourite island aesthetics to show you what's possible with a little imagination and a lot of hard work.

COTTAGECORE

This theme is all about being in harmony with nature and living the simple life. You'll need plenty of trees, farms and flowers, with lots of earthy tones. Avoid using straight lines and right angles – opt for natural terrain and non-linear paths instead.

Basically, if your grandma would like it, then it's probably cottagecore-appropriate – in fact, cottagecore is sometimes referred to as grandmacore. It's a fairly cluttered aesthetic so feel free to place lots of items.

FAIRYCORE

Fairycore shares a lot of common themes with cottagecore, but it is a subtly different aesthetic. Like cottagecore, it's all about celebrating nature, but it has more of a focus on magic, and tends to incorporate brighter colours. Imagine the magical forest in *A Midsummer Night's Dream* and you're on the right track.

Pinks, blues and purples work well for fairycore, and whimsical items like butterfly models make the perfect decor. Anything that glows in the dark or looks like it's been sprinkled with fairy dust will be perfect.

GOTHCORE

This is the perfect theme for those of you who find beauty in the darker side of life. Gothcore islands are nothing if not dramatic. They incorporate witchy motifs and items associated with death – graveyards and skeletons are common sights.

It should come as no surprise that the best colours for gothcore are black and purple, so get breeding those black hybrid flowers. Cedar trees help to create a spooky forest vibe, and a smattering of mushrooms will help give a dank, dark feel to your gothcore island.

BIG CITY

Being on a deserted island doesn't mean you can't enjoy a slice of city life. A big city aesthetic is easy enough to achieve, especially if you're good at creating custom design paths. If you want to go with this aesthetic, make sure you position everything in a grid layout and avoid any natural-looking terrain.

Focus on man-made, industrial items and avoid natural items like trees and flowers. You can get lots of city-appropriate items in exchange for Nook Miles – the utility pole, manhole cover and solar panel are all great choices. Make sure you add some bins for a truly authentic feel.

TROPICAL PARADISE

Picture the scene: you're on holiday in an exotic location, sipping a fruity drink and enjoying the relaxing sounds of the ocean. This can all be recreated in Animal Crossing with some well-chosen items and the perfect beachside location.

You'll want lots of palm trees, tiki torches, flamingos and coconut juice for this theme. Palm tree lamps and soft serve lamps are ideal light sources, and shell items also work well. If in doubt, find every bright, tropical item you can and set everything up at the edge of the beach.

PIRATE COVE

Thanks to Gullivarrr, there are now lots of pirate-themed items available to help you create the perfect pirate cove. There are barrels, treasure chests, cannons and all manner of pirate outfits to choose from. But you'll have to earn them first, of course!

A pirate-themed island is a popular choice with many in the Animal Crossing community, and the beaches are the perfect backdrop. This theme will feel tropical – tiki torches, coconut juice and palm trees will help to give your cove a Caribbean vibe. You can place bags of Bells to add to the treasure haul and work in any other nautical items you have to hand.

OUT OF THIS WORLD

Celestial objects play a big role in Animal Crossing, so it's no surprise that the celestial theme is very popular. This aesthetic is perfect for stargazing enthusiasts and aspiring astronauts alike – you can combine the space items with the star and zodiac items to create something that's truly out of this world.

This is a great theme to enjoy at night, since many of the objects light up. We'd recommend using the sand path for a lunar surface effect, but you could also download one of the incredible community-made lunar path design, or have a go at making your own.

DESERT ADVENTURE

The desert adventure aesthetic is sure to appeal to history lovers. The landscape is easy enough to create – just use your sand path to make a desert scene – but the decorative items are a little trickier to get hold of.

Anything gold or extravagant will work well for this theme, so make sure you have a good supply of gold nuggets for crafting. There are also several ancient objects that will do nicely, if you can get your hands on them – you can only obtain pyramids by helping Gulliver. Finally, pick a suitably dramatic outfit like the pharaoh outfit or the mummy outfit.

FIVE STAR ISLAND CHECKLIST

Everyone dreams of earning the coveted five star island rating. The better the balance of natural beauty, development and décor, the more stars your island will receive. With the help of this checklist, you'll have a five star island in no time.

1 PLANT TREES

Plant as many trees as you can, up to a maximum of 190. If you plant more than this, you won't get any extra points and it will become difficult to move around and place items. Isabelle will tell you if you have too many trees.

2 PLANT LOTS OF FLOWERS

This is an obvious one – the more flowers you have, the higher your island rating will be. Include a mixture of species and make sure to get plenty of hybrid colours in there, too. You can tuck flowers into small areas along cliffs and buildings so they don't get underfoot.

3 AVOID LITTERING

It's OK to drop the occasional item on the ground, but make sure you never drop more than fifteen items at once – any higher and your island is considered messy and will lose points. Dropped items include sticks which fall from trees, so make sure you tidy your island each day.

4

BUILD ALL BUILDINGS

This is another obvious one – make sure you have the museum, the Able Sisters shop and the expanded version of Nook's Cranny. These are key elements of any five star island, and they make everything more fun.

5

HAVE TEN RESIDENTS LIVING ON YOUR ISLAND

You'll need eight residents if you want to get a two star rating. If you're aiming for five stars, make sure every housing plot has been built and filled, and you have an island full of happy villagers just dying to leave positive feedback with Isabelle.

6

PLACE SOMETHING IN EACH AREA OF YOUR ISLAND

Think of your island as being divided into squares composed of 8 x 8 tiles. One tile is the size of a planted flower. You'll earn more points if you have items in each 8 x 8 square of your island, rather than in just a few areas, so make sure you decorate everywhere.

7 ADD BRIDGES

There's nothing five star about an island that's impossible to travel across, so make sure each piece of land is connected by bridges. Remember, you can have a maximum of eight bridges on your island at one time.

8. ADD INCLINES

You'll want to add inclines for the same reason you'll want to add bridges – they earn you points and help your fellow villagers move around the island. Make sure every high piece of land is accessible.

9. PLACE FENCES

Place fences around each building on your island to increase your island rating. The more fences you place, the more points you'll earn. Plus, it's nice for each of your villagers to have their own enclosed garden where they can spend some time alone.

10

PLACE DIY ITEMS

DIY items (items you have to craft) contribute to your island's scenery score, so make sure you display lots of them around your island. Variety is key – place lots of different items rather than the same few items over and over again.

11 PLACE NON-DIY ITEMS

Non-DIY items (items that can only be purchased or earned) are just as important as DIY items when it comes to your scenery score. Again, variety is key, so make sure you have a good range of pieces and display them all over your island. The more expensive the item, the more points you'll earn.

12

REMOVE WEEDS

If your island is covered in weeds, people will think you don't care, and your island will lose points. Keep an eye out for any stray tufts of grass and pull them up as soon as you see them. We want to see tidy, well-tended grass and flower beds!

13 FIVE STAR ISLAND REWARDS

Remember to keep checking in with Isabelle so you know what your current island rating is. When you finally make it to five stars, Isabelle will reward you with the recipe for a gold watering can. This valuable item is the only way to obtain gold roses – watering black roses with a gold watering can gives them a fifty percent chance of spawning a gold rose in the spot next to them. The other great thing about achieving five star island status is that the lily of the valley flower will begin to grow randomly on your island. This flower is very rare and can't be bought.

BUT WAIT! THERE'S MORE...

Well, that was fun! You should take a moment to congratulate yourself – you've come a long way since you first set foot on your island, and you've made Tom Nook very happy indeed. But the fun doesn't stop here – Animal Crossing is constantly being updated with new items, events and characters, so you'll be enjoying island life for a long time to come.

We hope this guide has helped inspire you to live your best island life. Just remember to make friends, be creative and have fun.

Enjoy!